INKLINGS
Poems of the Point and Beyond

Don Gutteridge

Black Moss
Press
2017

Library and Archives Canada Cataloguing in Publication

Gutteridge, Don, 1937-, author
     Inklings: poems of the point and beyond / Don Gutteridge.

ISBN 978-0-88753-581-9 (softcover)

     I. Title.

PS8513.U85I55 2017   C811'.54   C2017-903345-X

Cover image: Karakatsya
Design: Karen Veryle Monck

Thanks to Laurie Nicholson for typing the mss

 Black Moss Press
EST. 1969

Published by Black Moss Press
2450 Byng Road
Windsor, ON N8W 3E8 Canada

www.blackmosspress.com

Black Moss books are distributed in Canada and the U.S. by Fitzhenry & Whiteside. All orders should be directed there.

Black Moss Press acknowledges the support of the Canada Council for the Arts and the Ontario Arts Council for its publishing program.

 ONTARIO ARTS COUNCIL
CONSEIL DES ARTS DE L'ONTARIO

 Canada Council   Conseil des Arts
for the Arts   du Canada

PRINTED IN CANADA

Contents

PART THREE
Whatever

PART ONE

What Was

POET

It's Grade Seven and I'm
penning my first poem:
the epic clash of generals,
Wolfe and Montcalm squeezed
into the embracing rhythms
of a ballad, and me, no
skeptic, hero-worshipped
both men: self-
made, dashing, living
for history, cut in the heroic
mold and, I was quick
to note, doomed to a
theatrical death that set
my quill a-quiver, and who
cared if the quatrains were not
bold enough or the rhymes
unseasonable? I was a poet
and presumed to let the world
know it.

A WORLD AWAY

When I was young and the world
was a world away, I grew
as green as the grass on grand-
father's lawn, up-
right in my innocence
among lilacs and roses
that curled the edges of my
infant sight, and I
touched the tremor of trees
and felt seconds ticking
by and, for the first time,
something alien
burgeoning in the sun-
licked leafage, but I
had no quarrel then
with the passing of unweaned
winds or the mote in my mind's
eye, and no urge
to ask the world why.

DOOMED

Entombed in my bedroom
for seven months, I dreamt
of leaves enlivened by light
and lilacs on my grand-
father's hedge, but the more
I thought of the world outside
the deeper I delved into what
lay in my fancy and magnified
my imagination: I dwelt
on the thin edge of things,
where shadow and shape turned
into the inklings of plot and poem:
I danced in their delight, doomed
to write.

FATHOM

We boasted that our Lake was as big
as most oceans and as blue
as a heron's underwing
in serene sun, and older
than the Attawandaron who coveted
clams in its sandy shallows,
and when the wind rose
like Adam at first light,
waves as steep as cathedrals
thunder-plunged upon
the beaches where we paddled
and played porpoise:
feeling in the roiled white-
caps the throb of some-
thing deeper, the jolting
genesis of a thirst too
fathomed to be slaked.

GRACE

For Bob, In Loving Memory

You were my first audience,
listening in the dark between
our beds as I performed
my playlets, doing all
the voices like a slick-tongued
ventriloquist on the radio:
you laughed in the right places
and flicked a query or two:
"Is that Andy?" or "Might
it be Peewee?" and I yearned
for your approval and imagined
the applause we'd share when we
wrote down these joint
dramas; I still recall
those near-perfect
nights and your affable, loving
ear, given with such
brotherly grace.

LYRICAL

The grass on grandfather's
lawn surpassed the green
sheen of the Emerald Isle
and to my three-year-old
glance a place where goblins
were gobblesome and fairies
flitted faintly among
the lilacs that hemmed it in,
and where we somersaulted
on the humped hillock
like acrobatic imps,
and where the sun's while
embered in the two tall
trees like a small miracle
of light, and where to my surprise
and delight I first remember
seeing Grandpa's lyrical,
loving eyes.

THOUGHTS

On the ice-glazed fields
of Lecky's fallow lot
we skidded and skedadelled,
playing bump-the-body
tag and tumbling together
like cubs in a mother's den,
amazed at such cozy
contiguity, and if one part
of a forbidden bulge
accidentally bunted
another in the roly-poly
of the game, what the heck,
we were young, shamelessly
indulged, and kept our prurient
thoughts hidden.

POSSIBLE

When the Reverend Bell preached,
I almost believed, the hallowed
breath reaching all
the way to the nape of my neck,
but the imp in me left me
numb to the pastor's imperious
pleas to put me into the
Lord's capable hands,
until the day when his house
was blown to Kingdom Come,
and without a nod to Lady
Luck was found pell-mell
and bewildered on his front
lawn, pleased as the Great
Gildersleeve to be among
the living, and it struck me then
that there was possibly a God.

AFLOAT

Tom and I afloat
on the svelte swells of
Cameron Lake, trying
to baffle black bass
with our nautical know-how,
or, failing that, out-
witting a perch passing
through the deep dells
below: Tom at the prow,
manning the anchor, me
at the helm, easing
us into a cove where we fish
till the hour of the dying
day, snaffling a catch
or two, but mostly content
in one another's company,
nothing at stake but mutual
love, overwhelmed
by its compelling power.

BEND

We skated across the crisp
countryside under
a moon as pale as a beluga's
belly, as if we were skimming
Earth's meridian while the stars
inked the sky above
with all their unfrugality
and the wind sang like the
tremulo of a tenor sax,
and Grace and I in timeless
tandem whispered the ice
with our emboldened blades
until we reached the rink's
infinite end, and felt
the globe bend on its ancient
axis.

OOGA-OOGA

Herbie Gilbert loved
life and wanted the world
to know it: you could hear
his Tin Lizzie three
blocks away, as loud as a
drum-and-fife troop,
and should one happen
to stray too near,
he'd do a loop-de-loop
and hit the ooga-ooga
horn just to say "I'm here!
I'm me!" and we all
were tickled by the tintinnabulum
the old Ford made
as it sizzled on by,
going to beat the band –
and forlorn for Herbie
was a foreign land.

INCURABLE

When Mrs. Bradley screamed
her ear-curdling cry,
the whole village winced
at the full-throttled rage
whose only aim was outward
into a world convinced
she was mad, and wondering
what it must be like to lose
yourself inside yourself
and be deemed a captive
of your own incurable
old age.

FORBIDDEN

Whatever was forbidden
drew us towards it
like moths to a mammoth moon:
we were warned against The Slip,
too deep for dog-
paddling neophytes,
or hoboes with their anguished
eyes, or the Pool Room,
where we were addled by the
slick click of cue
on ball and the thwack of the
struck pocket (hidden
strictly from view), and we
wondered what shenanigans
our parents got up to
when the blinds came down,
or what strange terrain
was squeezed between the thighs
of girls we worshipped
from afar, too shy
to say hello or goodbye,
we rode our bikes double
to tease Pedan, our slew-
footed cop, and most
of all we dared the indelible
dark that each evening
enveiled our village –
a long ways East
of Eden.

TALLY-HO

When the harnessed heads of the
Clydes shook, music
tingled the star-startled
night above, and whiskered
hooves sped along the back-
country roads like Pegasus
preparing for flight, while on the
sled they whisked we cuddled
and bundled like would-be
lovers or raced along the furrowed
trail behind like kittinish
colts until, winded,
we caught up just
in time to alight before
swanning, eyes bright,
and fingers winter-bitten,
into the snow-rich ditch,
like spread-eagled angels,
while Miss Nelson, perched
on the bench beside our driver,
smiled as if some secret
remained untold:
of children a-glee and aglow
and singing, with the full voltage
of their voices, "Tally Ho!"

DINNER

Mrs. McCleister's rooster
serenaded our street the moment
the morning sun tickled
his wattle, and then paraded
among his hens, crowing
over every conquest,
loud enough to make
a village wince, and boost
his gallic ego, till
my grandmother, losing
her legendary patience,
threatened to throttle him
and make him the principal
guest at her Easter dinner.

QUARREL

Grandpa Shaving: 1946

First the hot towel
flush upon the face
I loved more than any
other, and I watched
the shaving cream as it whorled
in its blue bowl like a
rose unfolding in a
rush of new light,
and then the razor gliding
down each whiskered
cheek as smooth as a boy
like me on a toboggan
run, and up under
the chin with a flip
and a flare and a smile
for me, and a pat on the
noggin for my patient
patronage: my heart
hearkened, and at that moment
I was so enamoured of the world
I decided to end my quarrel
with it.

FOG

Point Edward: 1944

I lie safe in my bed
and hear the fog horn's
boom (oo-aah)
like a hippopotamus in pain,
a sound so loud I think
it haunts my very room,
and I picture the deck-hands,
fog-frazzled, peering
into the shrouded night
like blinded Argonauts:
"Steady as she goes!"
and when I finally fall
asleep, I dream of hippos
and a morning bedazzled
by sunlight.

WHAT WAS

In this photo my Gran
looks pensively towards
some future, chin high,
while the Sunday Jello
cools on the verandah
behind her: she has no
thoughts of church or its
self-serving sermonizing,
nor does the past intrude:
better forgotten the child
in the grit-endued streets
of central London and the mother
who was a lady of the night;
better remembered the family
who took her in, and safe
in Canada passed her off
as one of their own, a secret
kept for more than five
dozen years, and I'm left
wondering what courage it took
to abandon your home and say
hello to a far country,
but then I see it there
in her eyes, and I weep
for what was.

GOLDENROD

In the goldenrod daze
of September, we set out
like larcenous LaSalles
for the schoolhouse a mile
and a quarter away, along
a road garnished with gravel,
where puffs of dust beguile
our footsteps and we while
away the time spooking
sparrows from the rough
underbrush and some-
times a spray of cowbirds
who take flight as the girls
cry "My wedding!",
and we pass meadows
where Holsteins graze in the
heat-haze and huge-
hoofed horses plunder
the grass and toss their mutinous
manes as we nod to barn
after barn with silos
stuffed with fodder and stare
at the leaf-fringed woods: and there
on the horizon, hefting the sun
into a high sky, is our home-
for-the-day and all the days
and this awe-tinged autumn.

MOTIVE

Point Edward: 1948

The village that spawned me
and kept me cozy
for a dozen years, was pointless
(I searched for it one
day and came home
puzzled) and long ago
was a railway town
bustling with locomotives
and a switching yard, until,
like railroads everywhere,
they pulled up the tracks
and skedadelled, leaving
a single line to rust
away (and a village shrunken,
out-of-joint with the world),
a set of tracks we trod
on our way to Canatara
where the faithful
Lake was motive enough
for a day's play (while
the sun-nuzzled dunes
warmed us, where we clambered
on amber afternoons)
and the slow walk home
along those ties
where we felt the heft of history
and realized the point of it all.

ALIVE

For my Grandfather
In memoriam

How did you survive
three-and-a-half-years
in those trenches, riddled
with rats and drenched with shells
that shuddered the earth around you,
shorn of trees and the trilling
of biddable birds? Was it fear
that bolstered your blood? Did you
blench as that bullet struck
your bone? Did you mourn
those who succumbed on that
killing ground? Or were you
too numbed by bomb-
blast and machine-gun
stutter? Was there a moment
to dream of home and your son
still unseen, of lasting
things, of the sure hope
that somehow there might be
a future where you could thrive?
You do not answer (after all
what words could you utter?)
but I know that you lived
so I could be born alive.

LIGHT

For Dave Withers

Wiz Withers was a wizard
with wood, his crowning gift
to us was a racer worthy
of the Soap-Box Derby,
confected out of two
crates and four buggy
wheels, with twin ropes
to tug it left or right:
it was my honour to pole
it hither and thither
about the town, whose amazed
souls stood by and dusted
us with their applause; I think
of those intoxicating days
so long ago
whenever I need a moment's
memory to lift me
towards light.

AWASH

We couldn't afford skates
so we skidded on our galoshes
on Foster's frozen pond
like ducks on skinned ice
(no city-slicking
posh shin-pads
for us) with much-bruised
sticks bent like
boomerangs, awash in the
lithe light of a moon
as rotund as a gilded platter,
we chased the peregrinating
puck to and fro
and, with skates or no,
we played as if it mattered.

DAZZLED

Bonnie and Sharon hop-
scotching with their skirts thigh-
high in the biddable breeze,
while Johnny and Aaron play
rugby with a sturdy hurling
of the skin-tight ball:
the duos remain un-
frazzled by the other's id,
until, by and by,
the girls begin to flirt
and the boys enthrall,
each dazzled at its own
delight.

26

CHARLIE

Charlie was our neighbour,
a decorated vet who weathered
his nightmares with whiskey,
and, when that wouldn't do,
in beer binges at the Balmoral,
but nothing could unhinge
his image-riddled mind,
not even his three beautiful
daughters who doted on him
and us, and pretended not
to see that smile with the ache
in the middle.

NO ROOM

When you are just five
each day is a live
beginning: the sun rises
rosy over First Bush,
inundating it with light,
the streets shine, saying
"Walk on me, skip
on me!"; here, to your delight,
the wind does not gust,
it purrs; my village is as
cozy as a womb and I am
at ease being me in such
a place, where there is no
room for doom.

BEYOND MEASURE

We got much pleasure
watching the girls do
Double Dutch, the ropes
whispering the sidewalk
with rhythmic strokes as gentle
as a jazz trombone,
bare limbs frantically
exposed as one girl
glides in and another
out with pinpoint
precision, skirts flung
thighward, leaving us
dazzled, hopes high,
and envious beyond measure.

UNWILLING

When my Dad uprooted
us, moving me
from the only home I'd ever
known, my best friend
Butch, fulfilling a promise
he swore to, cycled
behind the moving van
all four miles to our
new abode, defying
the gravel-strewn county
road, unwilling
to say goodbye.

HOLY

For Gran: In Memoriam

In Sunday School we sang
as if God Himself
were keeping tabs, while
back home my Grandma
baked her weekly raisin
pies and watched her Jello
cool in its bowl on the side
verandah: I found it odd
that the Divine seldom visited
our abode, but there was affection
in those prized pies and more
love abiding there
than the Lord needed to keep
His Sabbath Holy.

ME

My grandfather endured
three-and-a-half years
in the lurid fields of Flanders,
burrowed in slit trenches
unfit for humans,
like some subterranean
beast, while the air rang
with the nickering whiz of bullets,
and shells flattened the furrows
of farms and cratered meadow-
lands whose trees were stripped
to sticks, and there was not
a bird who sang his breeding
song, and all those
horrific hours he would not
yield to death because
there was something
in every breath he took
that imagined home, imagined
family, imagined me.

DAZE

On sizzling summer nights
boys budding and girls
sudden with breasts play
hide-and-go-seek
in the juddering shadows
under the lascivious light
of a June moon: too
soon to be blessed by
some tremulous touch, they wait
for the "all free" call
and come running in side-
ways tandem towards
Mara's lamp and what
is just beginning to daze
and delight.

HEALED

When the fever finally broke,
the valves in my heart opened
like petals seized by the sun,
and I lay in my lonely bed
for seven long months
until they closed again
like lilies at the end of day,
and despite my mother's fears
my healed heart has kept
on beating for more than
seventy years.

BLAZE

For the Point Edward
volunteer firefighters

When the fire siren
assaulted the air over the
village, a dozen boys
vaulted onto their bikes
and trailed the roaring red
engine with big-muscled
men clinging on
like bos'uns on the rigging,
hoping for a blaze like the one
that levelled Burgess Market
or the gas-blast that blew
the Reverend Bell onto
his front lawn, but when
the spanking new truck
drew to a thankless halt
before a field no longer
smouldering in the heat-haze,
our hearts sank.

BADGE

And me the goalkeeper
in my prized shin-pads
(last year's Eatons),
sweeping pucks aside
until one of them surprises
my left eye, and to ease
the pain I imagine I am
Turk Broda taking
six stitches and playing
on: so I hitch up
my pads and wear my blackened
eye like a badge.

DUNES

The dunes of Canatara
are older than the Attawandaron
who wandered here in search
of freshwater clams
under a night sky
trembling with stars and a
miraculous moon,
and as dawn assembled itself
on a prism-rich horizon,
they lay themselves
down on the sun-drenched
hillocks and dreamt of
Gichimanitou and sturgeon
stalwart enough to feed
a village.

PART TWO

What Now

SUNDAY WALK

Grandpa and I
on our Sunday walk,
circumnavigating our village,
me firing question
after question and he
answering them as if I were
some sort of Socrates;
we skirt the marsh, its grasses
stalk-dry, the cattails
shredding in the June breeze,
the air lavish with light;
his corporal's stride is shortened
for my stutter-step as we reach
First Bush, busy
with bees and birdsong,
and we find a kind of furtive
joy in taking the long
route home, and I try
not to hear some terminal
clock ticking time
away from the love neither
of us needs to utter.

WHATEVER GROWS
For Anne

You were born with a green
thumb, and ever since
everything you've touched
has sprouted, budded or blossomed:
roses that tumble on their trellises,
petunia pots showering
our porch with a blaze of petals,
forget-me-nots
fringing the lawn with the
sprightliness of Spring:
you are a daughter of Demeter,
a dean of whatever
grows, and you are un-
amazed at your own delight.

SMILE
For Lilly Hall McWatters
In Memoriam

All I have left of my maternal
grandmother is this
framed photo, out of which,
bereft of breath and stiffened
with a pinch of pride she pins
me with a Presbyterian
eye, as if measuring the mettle
of the grandson she would never
know, and how I wish
she had lived another three
years so we could have met
face to face, in fine
fettle, my chubby guile-
less presence widening
her smile.

38

IRISH

My mother's father built
the bloated mansions along
the London Road with hammer,
saw and chisel, his eye
as true as a cartographer's
sighting his sextant on a distant
star, and when the job
was done, he'd dance a jig
at the next bar, until
the day he was murdered (before
I was two) at a bootlegger's
"ginger ale" party,
so I don't remember him
dandling me on his knee
or doting on the firstborn,
for I hadn't yet grown into
the boy who would laugh at his tall
tales or his Gaelic wit;
instead, with his untimely
demise, I pen this poem,
and dedicate it to his Irish
eyes.

NINE YEARS

For Potsy: In Memoriam

It's been nine long years
since you left us,
nine years bereft of your rough
love or those amber
afternoons we spent
on fairways and greens
(where the arc of your swing
hummed like a Turk's scimitar)
or the summers at Cameron Lake,
the two of us passionate
about perch or the odd black
bass you landed with ample
aplomb: nine years
without those luncheons
where I sat surprised
and aglow at the stories you spun
about your prized days
in the War, nine long
years, and I still haven't
forgiven God for your passing.

FIRST STEPS
For Tom

It must have taken the courage
of a lion in his pride for you
to step into the terrifying emptiness
of air, that vacancy
of space, without ballast
or handhold, one
tentative toe at a time,
bracing against some
notion of balance
upright in your mind;
you smile at me, arms
outstretched, as you hit
your stride and fall
delighted into my embrace:
these are moments that last,
lingering in the manifold
layers of memory.

FANCY
For Ivy

You do a song-and-dance
for us, prancing about
like a pixie with foot-
bobbing ease, and all
the time telling us
a tale of two bunnies
hopping into the morning
sunshine: one eye
fixed on the story that grips
you deep down where
fancy and the imagination
lie.

CONNOISSEUR

For Amanda

You are a connoisseur
of fruit pies and raisin-
puffed muffins, and you
bring this lufting touch
to the clinic, where cats purr
at your approach and dogs
lick your face with doggy
delight, but most of all
you are yourself, comfortable
in your own skin and self-
effacing to a fault: may the world
light up your life.

IRIS

For Becky

If you were a flower you'd be
a water iris, deep-
rooted, its slender blue
beauty above the silken
surface of a pond: O
daughter, we love your fiery
spirit, your tender heart,
your acts of kindness,
your selfless service,
of which at every passing
hour we grow more fond.

42

ALLURE
Guelph 1960: For Anne

What I remember most
is the Volkswagon with the
sun-roof eased
open, and you in your lemon-
yellow dress, red
hair a-flair in the autumnal
breeze, your eyes as blue
as the underbelly of the sky:
you coasted up to the curb
where I was waiting, trying
not to look surprised,
and so mesmerized was I
by your allure, I must confess
I wasn't sure whether I loved
you, the car or the dress.

PUCK
For Jeff

If you were a flower, you'd be
a jack-in-the-pulpit,
your imp's grin tucked
into respectably purple
whorls, you are Shakespeare's
Puck on his lucky day,
your Falstaffian laugh
would make a cat purr:
we love your free spirit,
your Harry Potter panache,
and that you had the good
sense to marry my daughter:
you swallow the world in one
gulp.

MAPLE

For Kevin

If you were a tree you'd be
a maple with leaves as soft
as flags flying aloft
of Parliament and a grain
as gritty as the sap is supple:
we love your wit and gentle
way with all who come
within your compass,
you are as impish as you are
disarming: may the gods
of graciousness be with you
every golden day.

LABYRINTHS

My girls gather about
their grandmother like chicks
hedging a hen, creating
crafts she demonstrates
with fingers affixed to arts
learned long ago and now,
hand-in-glove, passed
down during these
amiable afternoons,
when something rather
deeper is dredged up
from the labyrinths of love.

44

MAGIC

Cameron Lake is a pellucid
blue, and Tom and I
cavort in its chill welcome
like tantalizing tortoises:
now lolling on our plastic
mattresses, now diving
like deft dolphins or orphaned
Orcas, and when we've had
our fill, we lie upon
the sun-saturated sand
and let the wind dry
us benign, certain
that this magical moment
will be everlasting.

COUPLED

Our love is now autumnal
and so it is we summon
up those days
when our love blossomed
like a bride's rose under
a supple sun and we looked
lovingly into the other's eye
for certitude and consolation
(our serendipity Heaven-sent),
and such thoughts, dazed
with delight, keep on
idling us into our age:
coupled and content.

WHEN I GO

When I go, do not
grieve me, for I shall leave
this world alive in the eyes
of those who've prized me
and helped me thrive so
long in a place where regret
can cripple without affection
and unfettered love;
I have done everything
I longed to: fathered
children and grandchildren,
found my life's love early
and ever, composed
poems and stories to keep
my patient peers amused,
and practised pedagogical
pentameters on unwitting
high-schoolers, and so
I ask you not to mourn,
for I will not have died:
I'll simply have run out
of words.

WITHIN

For years too numerous
to mention, we've been a duo,
unsingled when we were young
enough to love without qualm
or question, when our lips
tingled with anticipation,
and now we glide into our age,
becalmed and pleased
at having been, and if
perchance some blip
should startle our luminous love,
we say to one another:
"Open the ears of your heart
and listen to the music within."

PINE

For James

If you were a tree you'd be
a northern pine, stout
and stalwart, steady
in the stiffest breeze:
you put the gentle into gentlemen,
you fly your flags un-
furled, strictly yourself,
and doubtless ready
to ease the pain of others
or be the one to help:
may the gods be with you
as you sally forth into an
unpredictable world.

WHEN I WAKE UP

When I wake up
after my demise, I'll be
surprised to find the world
and its will have moved on
without my approval,
though perhaps a story,
even a poem or two,
will linger in the minds of those
who care enough to plunge
into my plots or un-intricate
a metaphor before Time
expunges them all:
O it's not glory I'm after
in any guise, just a nod
or so from a merciful God
to justify my having been.

WORTHWHILE

For James and Tim

My grandsons long ago
in this photo tease
the front seat of my Ford
Tempo, and their bountiful
smiles at the camera's eye
are at ease in a way only
the young and infinitely innocent
can be, and I regret
all the years that have passed
between then and a miraculous
moment that made my life
worthwhile.

HOME

Point Edward: June 2016
For Gene Burdenuk

We navigate the streets
and lanes I trod all
those years ago,
the houses, whose every eave
and ell I know by heart,
leap out at me
whole, as if Time were a temporary
intrusion, and at every corner
a memory stirs, prodded
by the radium of recognition,
the River flats, where I cavorted
with kites, still greet
the world with their gratuitous green,
my grandfather's place,
remains, then as now,
a wide-verandahed
abode, where love abided,
and Mara's lamp, sadly
departed, glows still
in my childhood mind,
and in its honour I write
this poem of home.

PART THREE

Whatever

EMBRACE

For Gerald Parker

You are like a character
out of Commedia Delle' Arte,
Harlequin perhaps with his imp's
eyes and cherubic cheeks
that framed a Puckish
smile: you coaxed a generation
of students to dote on drama
and tease the meaning out of
Wallace Stevens, we loved
the way your fretful fingers
skittered over the black
keys and filled our living
room with mirthful music,
and O how we admired
your dot-dainty, elfin-
elegant paintings: you embraced
the world, playing your part,
and it has embraced you back.

INKLING

An inkling is a tingle
in the brain, a sprout abruptly
unbudded, the beginning
of a word or more precisely
its first singing syllable,
enticed towards a phrase,
and then by some urge
to say the unsayable,
the nub of a poem just
begun, and compelled
with a single-minded surge
to completion.

THE OTHER

A life unleavened
by love is not worth
living, we spend our days
reaching for reciprocity,
the singular pair of eyes,
lustrous with light,
into which we pour our trust
and all we have to give,
no Heaven can proffer
us more, no
deity teach us
more about our dazed
delight in the other.

WRITTEN

My words peregrinate
from my pen to the unscathed
page, wringing words
out of the whiteness there,
I let them purr or rage,
give them full rein,
let them sing whatever
song they are smitten with,
for I do not write:
I am written.

GOOD

Adam and Mistress Eve
have taken the fall for tasting
the fruit forbidden and un-
dappling the Garden; Eve
in particular is on the hook
for letting Evil into the world
to tarnish hearth and neighbourhood,
forgetting that half of Eve's
apple was garnished with Good.

BEAVER MEADOW

It comes upon you sudden,
unintimidated by the bush
that hems it in, a sweet
sway of sun-seething
grasses that welcomes you
after a long, fevered trudge
through the splay of branches
and tipped trunks, the place
where peace is more than a
word – bequeathed to us
by the unwitting labour
of the dam-derelict beaver.

VERACITY

A poem is not a thought,
it is, at first, the inkling
of some meaning in search
of words, still unwrought,
at odds with the world, until
some will distils
the lot and fashions a home
for rhythm and rhyme to peregrinate
into the veracity of verse.

BLUSH

It was just a crush to soften
the summer between seasons,
but desire knows no reason
when a rush of blood hums
near the heart: we circled
our block as often as the world
allows, hands enfolded,
our thoughts lofty, afire
with love's first blush.

SWEET SWING
For Ken Cooper

For twenty-odd years
I watched your sweet swing
with its air-arrowing arc
and frantic follow-through,
and observed with awe the way
you caressed a putt into the
cup, and then the shy
gentleman's grin as our cheers
greeted you: in your heyday
you could make a drive behave
as if it were struck by God
Himself, you could make a golf
ball sing.

AFFIRMED

After a reading at Mykanos
Restaurant in London, Ontario

There is a murmuring in the crowd
at Mykonos, all eyes
upon the ageing poet
as he grasps the lectern
and steadies himself under
the bright stage-light,
and, as those in their seats wait
to be wowed, words
drip off the bard's lips
in the sheer shape of poems,
rhymed or not, he reads
with surprising alliterative
ease, then nods at the sudden
outbursts of applause,
at the oohs and ahs in just
the right places, he smiles
a septuagenarian smile
in gratitude at something
significant having been affirmed.

PURVEYOR

For Ian Underhill

You spent a lifetime
purveying poems and stories
to generations of students,
reading aloud with alliterative
ease in your sturdy baritone
until the rhymes chimed
and the consonants collaborated,
until the metaphors stood
up and mentioned their meaning:
you gave them Munro and Purdy,
Atwood and Lawrence,
and all you asked for in return
was their passionate attention
and some small acknowledgement
that teachers, ungloried
as they are, really matter.

WILL

For Colm O'Sullivan
In Memoriam

You die surrounded by your family,
those who loved you best,
you summon up your penultimate
breath to utter the word
goodbye in flawless
Erse, your home-tongue,
as sweet upon the lips
as the haunted hills of Erin,
and I wonder which of the million
thoughts you saved for last,
perhaps some gem culled
from your joust with Joyce, or one
of those that linger long
in the minds of those who still
mourn your passionate passing,
and let it be said of such
a man, present or past,
he went with a will.

HALF

If I could grasp but half
a lifetime, it would be
the years when poetry flowed
with iambic ease and stories
pleased their way onto the page,
their words, like aspens, quivering
with impious import
upon the immaculate page,
and those I loved surrounded
me with effortless affection
and made the days glow:
no thoughts then
that I was not ageless
and that the poems would never
cease their daffidilian daze.

INNOCENCE

The petunias in God's Garden
were as pink as a bride's blush
and Adam drew his mate
towards their lush presence,
while the cobra-tongued intruder
slithered into Eden, and Eve,
unaware of her own
tempting beauty, stood
blinking in the succulent sun
at Adam's side, while he,
exempt from passion, found
himself unable
to crush the grasping asp
underfoot, and so
were lost, the last of the petunias,
the Garden, and innocence.

JURY

It's been a long and satisfying
life, and I intend to go
gently into Dylan's Good
Night: after all,
I've had my day, weaned
my soul from strife and woe,
eased myself into age
like a lark lifting into air,
content with what has been
allotted me, but the jury's
still out: as the last lick
of light flickers in the dark,
I may shout "Nay!" – bent
by bravado, fuelled by fury.

ABOUT THE AUTHOR

Don Gutteridge was born in Sarnia, Ontario and raised in the nearby village of Point Edward. He graduated from Western University with an Honours English degree and taught high school for seven years before moving to Western's Faculty of Education. There he taught English Methods for twenty-five years. He is the author of more than fifty books: poetry, fiction and scholarly works in educational theory and practice. In 1970 he won The UWO President's Medal for his poem "Death at Quebec." His collection *Coppermine* was a finalist for the 1973 Governor General's Award. He is currently Professor Emeritus and lives in London Ontario with his wife Anne.